CREATIVE  TOUCHES™

Painted Designs ETC.

THE HOME DECORATING INSTITUTE®

Copyright© 1996 Cy DeCosse Incorporated 5900 Green Oak Drive Minnetonka, Minnesota 55343
1-800-328-3895 All rights reserved Printed in U.S.A.

Library of Congress Cataloging-in-Publication Data Painted designs etc. p. cm. — (Creative touches)
Includes index. ISBN 0-86573-999-4 (softcover) 1. House painting. 2. Furniture painting. 3. Interior decoration. I. Cy DeCosse Incorporated. II. Series.
TT323.P32 1996 745.7 — dc20 96-26995

CONTENTS

Getting Started

Guided Designs

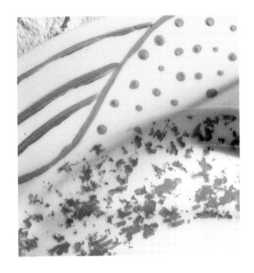

Freehand Designs

Painted Designs
ETC.

Decorate with personal style, using painted designs throughout your home. There are no limits to the designs and applications, nor to the enjoyment and satisfaction you'll receive.

Many sources offer inspiration for designs that can be painted as they are, or adapted to fit any space. Learn easy methods for enlarging or reducing designs and for transferring guidelines to the painting surface. Discover the tricks for painting perfect stripes and plaids on walls, furniture, and accesssories.

For a unique look, paint a surface with freehand designs. Try any of the designs suggested here, or use them as a springboard to creating your own personal designs. Embellish any surface, including ceramics and fabric, with freehand painted designs.

Be inspired by colorful step-by-step photography, the hallmark of the Creative Touches series.

GETTING STARTED

Primers & Finishes

PRIMERS

Some surfaces must be coated with a primer before the paint is applied. Primers ensure good adhesion of paint and are used to seal porous surfaces so paint will spread smoothly without soaking in. It is usually not necessary to prime a nonporous surface in good condition, such as smooth, unchipped, previously painted wood or wallboard. Many types of water-based primers are available; select one that is suitable for the type of surface you are painting.

A. FLAT LATEX PRIMER is used for sealing unfinished wallboard. It makes the surface nonporous so fewer coats of paint are needed. This primer may also be used to seal previously painted wallboard before you apply new paint of a dramatically different color. The primer prevents the original color from showing through.

B. LATEX ENAMEL UNDERCOAT is used for priming most raw woods or woods that have been previously painted or stained. A wood primer closes the pores of the wood, for a smooth surface. It is not used for cedar, redwood, or plywoods that contain water-soluble dyes, because the dyes would bleed through the primer.

C. RUST-INHIBITING LATEX METAL PRIMER helps paint adhere to metal. Once a rust-inhibiting primer is applied, water-based paint may be used on metal without causing the surface to rust.

D. POLYVINYL ACRYLIC PRIMER, or PVA, is used to seal the porous surface of plaster and unglazed pottery, if a smooth paint finish is desired. To preserve the texture of plaster or unglazed pottery, apply the paint directly to the surface without using a primer.

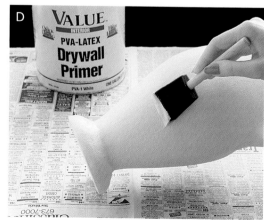

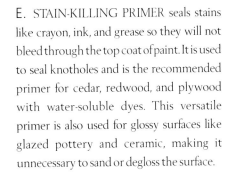

E. STAIN-KILLING PRIMER seals stains like crayon, ink, and grease so they will not bleed through the top coat of paint. It is used to seal knotholes and is the recommended primer for cedar, redwood, and plywood with water-soluble dyes. This versatile primer is also used for glossy surfaces like glazed pottery and ceramic, making it unnecessary to sand or degloss the surface.

FINISHES

Finishes are sometimes used over paint as the final coat. They protect the painted surface with a transparent coating. The degree of protection and durability varies, from a light application of matte aerosol sealer to a glossy layer of clear finish.

F. CLEAR FINISH, such as water-based urethanes and acrylics, may be used over painted finishes for added durability. Available in matte, satin, and gloss, these clear finishes are applied with a brush or sponge applicator. Environmentally safe clear finishes are available in pints, quarts, and gallons (0.5, 0.9, and 3.8 L) at paint supply stores and in 4-oz. and 8-oz. (119 and 237 mL) bottles or jars at craft stores.

G. AEROSOL CLEAR ACRYLIC SEALER, available in matte or gloss, may be used as the final coat over paint as a protective finish. A gloss sealer also adds sheen and depth to the painted finish for a more polished look. Apply aerosol sealer in several light coats rather than one heavy coat, to avoid dripping or puddling. To protect the environment, select an aerosol sealer that does not contain harmful propellants. Use all sealers in a well-ventilated area.

Tools & Supplies

TAPES

When painting, use tape to mask off any surrounding areas. Several brands are available, varying in the amount of tack, how well they release from the surface without damaging the base coat, and how long they can remain in place before removal. You may want to test the tape before applying it to the entire project. The edge of the tape should be sealed tightly to prevent seepage.

PAINT ROLLERS

Paint rollers are used to paint an area quickly with an even coat of paint. Roller pads, available in several nap thicknesses, are used in conjunction with roller frames. Use synthetic or lamb's wool roller pads to apply water-based paints.

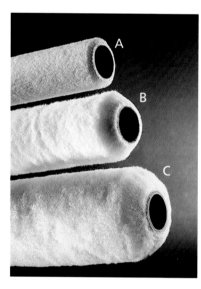

A. SHORT-NAP ROLLER PADS with 1/4" to 3/8" (6 mm to 1 cm) nap are used for applying glossy paints to smooth surfaces like wallboard, wood, and smooth plaster.

B. MEDIUM-NAP ROLLER PADS with 1/2" to 3/4" (1.3 to 2 cm) nap are used as all-purpose pads. They give flat surfaces a slight texture.

C. LONG-NAP ROLLER PADS with 1" to 1 1/4" (2.5 to 3.2 cm) nap are used to cover textured areas in fewer passes.

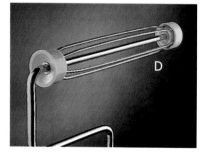

D. ROLLER FRAME is the metal arm and handle that holds the roller pad in place. A wire cage supports the pad in the middle. Select a roller frame with nylon bearings so it will roll smoothly and a threaded end on the handle so you can attach an extension pole.

E. EXTENSION POLE has a threaded end that screws into the handle of a roller frame. Use an extension pole when painting ceilings, high wall areas, and floors.

PAINTBRUSHES & APPLICATORS

Several types of paintbrushes and applicators are available, designed for various purposes. Select the correct one to achieve the best quality in the paint finish.

A. SYNTHETIC-BRISTLE paintbrushes are generally used with water-based latex and acrylic paints, while B. NATURAL-BRISTLE brushes are used with alkyd, or oil-based paints. Natural-bristle paintbrushes may be used with water-based paints to create certain decorative effects.

C. BRUSH COMBS remove dried or stubborn paint particles from paintbrushes and align the bristles so they dry properly. To use a brush comb, hold the brush in a stream of water as you pull the comb several times through the bristles from the base to the tips. Use mild soap on the brush, if necessary, and rinse well. The curved side of the tool can be used to remove paint from the roller pad.

Stencil brushes are available in a range of sizes. Use the small brushes for fine detail work in small stencil openings, and the large brushes for larger openings. Either D. SNYTHETIC or E. NATURAL-BRISTLE stencil brushes may be used with acrylic paints.

Artist's brushes are available in several types, including F. FAN, G. LINER, and H. FLAT BRUSHES. After cleaning the brushes, always reshape the head of the brush by stroking the bristles with your fingers. Store artist's brushes upright on their handles or lying flat so there is no pressure on the bristles.

I. SPONGE APPLICATORS are used for a smooth application of paint on flat surfaces.

J. PAINT EDGERS with guide wheels are used to apply paint next to moldings, ceilings, and corners. The guide wheels can be adjusted for proper alignment of the paint pad.

Preparing the Surface

To achieve a high-quality and long-lasting paint finish that adheres well to the surface, it is important to prepare the surface properly so it is clean and smooth. The preparation steps vary, depending on the type of surface you are painting. Often it is necessary to apply a primer to the surface before painting it. For more information about primers, refer to pages 8 and 9.

PREPARING SURFACES FOR PAINTING

SURFACE TO BE PAINTED	PREPARATION STEPS	PRIMER
UNFINISHED WOOD	1. Sand surface to smooth it. 2. Wipe with damp cloth to remove grit. 3. Apply primer.	Latex enamel undercoat.
PREVIOUSLY PAINTED WOOD	1. Clean surface to remove any grease and dirt. 2. Rinse with clear water; allow to dry. 3. Sand surface lightly to degloss and smooth it and to remove any loose paint chips. 4. Wipe with damp cloth to remove grit. 5. Apply primer to any areas of bare wood.	Not necessary, except to touch up areas of bare wood; then use latex enamel undercoat.
PREVIOUSLY VARNISHED WOOD	1. Clean surface to remove any grease and dirt. 2. Rinse with clear water; allow to dry. 3. Sand surface to degloss it. 4. Wipe with damp cloth to remove grit. 5. Apply primer.	Latex enamel undercoat.
UNFINSHED WALLBOARD	1. Dust with hand broom, or vacuum with soft brush attachment. 2. Apply primer.	Flat latex primer.
PREVIOUSLY PAINTED WALLBOARD	1. Clean surface to remove any grease and dirt. 2. Rinse with clear water; allow to dry. 3. Apply primer, only if making a dramatic color change.	Not necessary, except when painting over dark or strong color; then use flat latex primer.
UNPAINTED PLASTER	1. Sand any flat surfaces as necessary. 2. Dust with hand broom, or vacuum with soft brush attachment.	Polyvinyl acrylic primer.
PREVIOUSLY PAINTED PLASTER	1. Clean surface to remove any grease and dirt. 2. Rinse with clear water; allow to dry thoroughly. 3. Fill any cracks with spackling compound. 4. Sand surface to degloss it.	Not necessary, except when painting over dark or strong color; then use polyvinyl acrylic primer.
UNGLAZED POTTERY	1. Dust with brush, or vacuum with soft brush attachment. 2. Apply primer.	Polyvinyl acrylic primer or gesso.
GLAZED POTTERY, CERAMIC & GLASS	1. Clean surface to remove any grease and dirt. 2. Rinse with clear water; allow to dry thoroughly. 3. Apply primer.	Stain-killing primer.
METAL	1. Clean surface with vinegar or lacquer thinner to remove any grease and dirt. 2. Sand surface to degloss it and to remove any rust. 3. Wipe with damp cloth to remove grit. 4. Apply primer.	Rust-inhibiting latex metal primer.
FABRIC	1. Prewash fabric without fabric softener to remove any sizing, if fabric is washable. 2. Press fabric as necessary.	None.

Water-based Paints

A wide variety of paint is available from paint supply stores and craft stores. Each type has advantages that make it especially suitable for certain kinds of painting. All of the following are water-based, making cleanup easy with soap and water. Water-based paints are also safer for the environment than oil-based paints.

LATEX PAINTS

Latex paint is fast drying and durable. In addition to the wide range of premixed colors, latex paint can be custom-mixed by a paint professional. It is available in various finishes, from flat latex for a matte appearance to high-gloss latex with maximum sheen. Low-luster latex enamel paint, sometimes referred to as eggshell enamel, has some sheen and provides good coverage; semigloss has a bit more sheen. The glossier the paint, the more durable it is. Packaged in pints, quarts, and gallons (0.5, 0.9, and 3.8 L), latex paint is suitable for general use in small and large jobs.

Latex paint contains acrylic or vinyl resins or a combination of both. Latex paints of acrylic resins are the highest quality, with vinyl-acrylic blends next in quality, followed by paints consisting solely of vinyl resins. High-quality paints may cost significantly more, but they provide an even, complete coverage and wear longer.

CRAFT ACRYLIC PAINT

Craft acrylic paint contains 100 percent acrylic resins. Generally sold in 2-oz., 4-oz., and 8-oz. (59, 119, and 237 mL) bottles or jars, these premixed acrylics have a creamy brushing consistency and give excellent coverage. They should not be confused with the thicker artist's acrylics used for canvas paintings. Craft acrylic paint can be diluted with water, acrylic extender, or latex paint conditioner if a thinner consistency is desired. Craft acrylic paints are available in many colors and in metallic, fluorescent, and iridescent formulas.

CERAMIC PAINTS

Ceramic paints provide a scratch-resistant and translucent finish. They can be heat-hardened in a low-temperature oven to improve their durability, adhesion, and water resistance. Latex and acrylic paints may also be used for painting ceramics, provided the surface is properly primed (page 13).

FABRIC PAINTS

Fabric paints have been formulated specifically for painting on fabric. To prevent excessive stiffness in the painted fabric, avoid a heavy application; the texture of the fabric should show through the paint. Once the paints are heat-set with an iron, the fabric can be machine washed and dry-cleaned. Acrylic paints can also be used for fabric painting; textile medium may be added to the acrylics to make them more pliable on fabric.

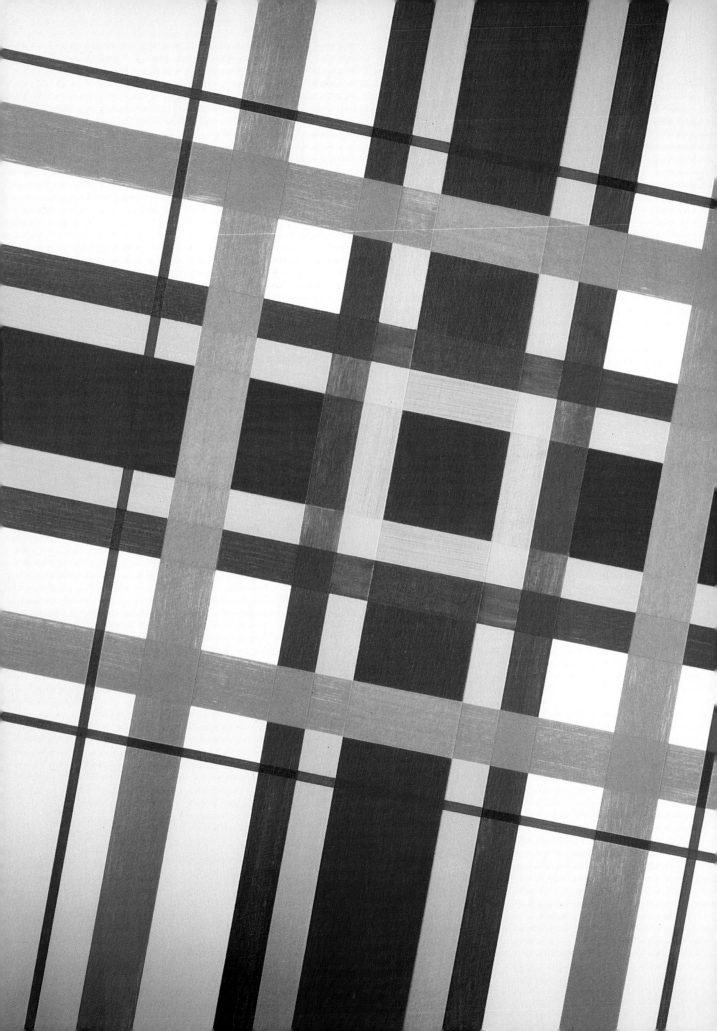

GUIDED DESIGNS

Inspiration for Designs

Inspiring ideas for creating designs can be found by looking closely at the shapes, colors, and textures around you. You may want to paint simple floral patterns that mimic those found in nature. Or adapt a wallpaper design to paint on coordinating curtains.

To help you decide which designs will work best for you, think about the descriptive words that define your personal tastes and decorating style. For example, if you describe your style as light, airy, and feminine, try a free-form floral design in pastels. For a design that is tailored, rich, and warm, choose a plaid in deep, inviting colors. For a look that is bright, bold, and clean, you may want to use a contemporary design with strong diagonal lines.

Look through ornamental design books, available at local libraries and bookstores, usually located in the art section. Study the ethnic patterns found on fabrics and accessories, like those on woven rugs and glazed pots. Clip photos from magazines. Even the advertisements in magazines feature the latest colors and patterns in fabrics and furnishings.

NATURE provides both shape and color ideas. Autumn leaves inspire simple free-form designs.

Continued

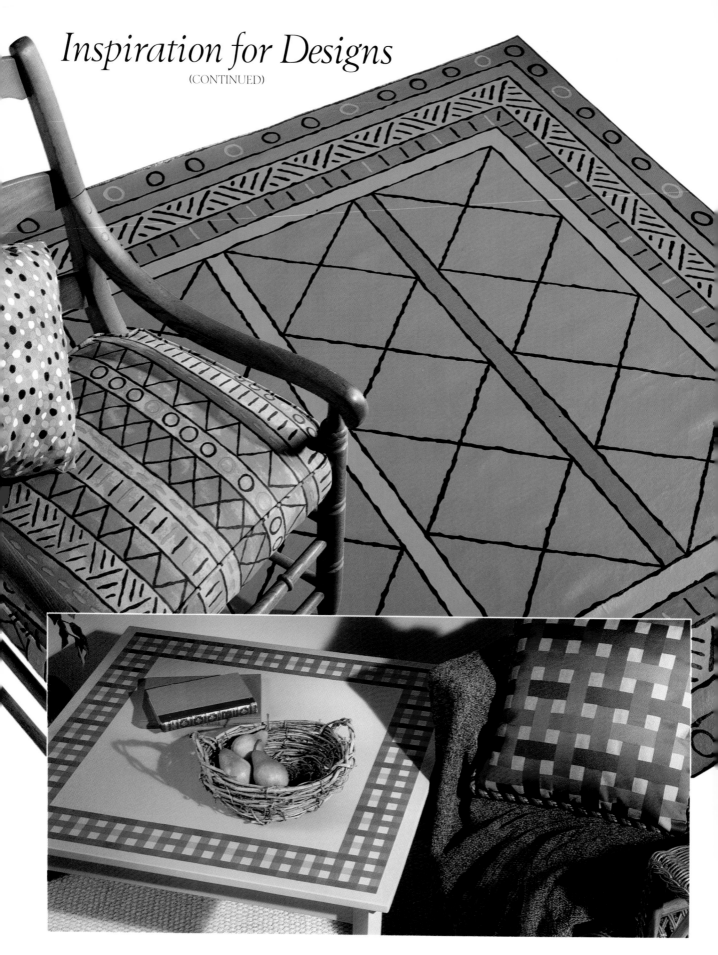

OPPOSITE, TOP: GEOMETRIC FABRIC DESIGN was mimicked to create a coordinating floor cloth.

OPPOSITE, BOTTOM: PLAID FABRIC inspired the bold design for the tabletop. The design was painted using evenly spaced rows of painter's masking tape as a guide.

ABOVE: WALLCOVERING BORDER is used for creating the stenciled design on the small wooden chest.

BELOW: DESIGN BOOKS offer a wide selection of designs. A contemporary geometric design appears on a stylized pitcher.

Transferring Designs

For painted designs, you will often want to mark the design onto the surface after the base coat is applied. Designs can be transferred from wallcoverings, fabrics, books, and any other sources of inspiration (page 19), following a few simple techniques.

The first step in transferring a design is to duplicate it onto paper. To do this, you can cover the design with tracing paper and trace the design lines with a pencil. Hold the covered design up to a light source, such as a sunlit window or a light table, to see the design lines more clearly. A temporary light table can easily be made by placing a light under a glass-top table. As you trace the design, you may want to simplify it for easier painting, omitting fine or unnecessary details. To enlarge or reduce a design, use the grid method to draw the design to scale.

For many designs, a photocopy machine works well to eliminate the need for drawing the design, although any shaded areas in the original design will be copied, and the design will not be simplified. The design may be enlarged or reduced by using a photocopy machine that is set to a larger or smaller percentage of the original.

The design is transferred from the paper to the surface that will be painted, using graphite paper and tracing around the design with a pencil. The graphite lines on the surface mark the placement of the design; they may be erased after the design is painted.

How to enlarge or reduce a design using the grid method

1. Measure the length of original design, and decide on the desired finished length; this determines the sizes of the grids. For example, graph paper with a ¼" (6 mm) grid can be used to mark the original design; for the enlarged design, use paper with a ¾" (2 cm) grid to triple the size, as indicated by red lines.

2. Place graph paper over original design; trace design onto graph paper.

3. Look at original design, and draw design lines within each grid to scale on grid for the finished size.

How to enlarge a design using the photocopy method

1. Draw lines vertically and horizontally through design if finished size of design will no longer fit on a single sheet of paper.

2. Photocopy each area of the design, with the machine set at desired percentage of the original. Continue to make enlarged copies, using the previous copy of each area, until desired size is reached.

3. Trim copies along marked lines; tape sections together to make full-size design.

4. Redraw design lines on tracing paper, if necessary for clarity.

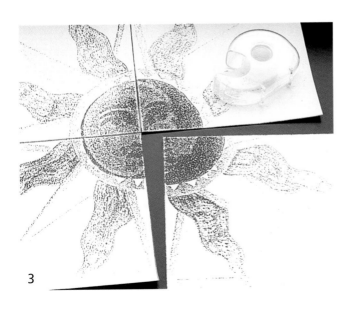

How to reduce a design using the photocopy method

1. Draw lines vertically and horizontally through design if original size of the design does not fit on single sheet of paper that can be used in the photocopy machine. Cut design apart on marked lines.

2. Photocopy each area of the design, with the machine set at desired percentage of the original. Darken lines, if necessary.

3. Continue to make reduced copies, using the previous copy of each area.

4. Trim copies along marked lines; tape sections together to make full-size design.

How to transfer a design for painting

1. Omit this step and step 2, if photocopied design is being used. Place tracing paper over design; work on a lighted surface, if design lines are difficult to see. To keep the design from shifting, tape it to a flat surface; this is especially helpful when tracing designs from fabric.

2. Trace around prominent design lines; simplify design, if desired, by omitting any fine details that would be too difficult or time-consuming to paint. Enlarge or reduce the design, if desired, using grid method on page 24.

3. Place photocopied or traced design over a sheet of graphite paper, with graphite side down; tape in desired position on surface to be painted. Outline the design, using pencil, to transfer the design to the surface.

Taped-off Designs

Simple techniques using painter's masking tape can help you create exacting patterns like plaids, stripes, and other geometric designs. Select a tape that prevents the paint from seeping underneath and is easily removed without damage to the base coat (page 10). Also, take care not to thin the paint too much and to apply the paint in light coats.

For stripes, use the painter's masking tape to divide the surface into parallel rows for precise painting. For plaid designs, the rows for the plaid are masked off and painted, one color at a time, first in one direction, then in the opposite direction.

How to paint a striped design

MATERIALS

• Painter's masking tape in desired width or widths.

• Latex or craft acrylic paints.

• Paintbrush or paint roller.

• Striped fabric, optional, for inspiration.

1. Apply base coat in desired color. Allow to dry.

2. Mark a light plumb line, using pencil and carpenter's level, if painting a design on a wall. Align the painter's masking tape for first stripe to the plumb line, pressing the edges of the tape firmly.

3. Measure and position parallel rows of masking tape for first stripe color, pressing edges firmly. Paint stripes of this color. Allow to dry.

4. Remove masking tape from previous steps. Apply rows of tape for next color; apply paint, and allow to dry. Repeat for any remaining colors.

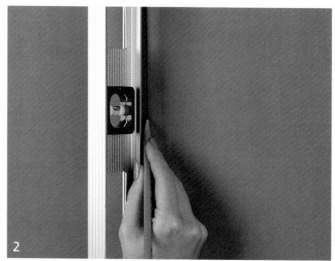

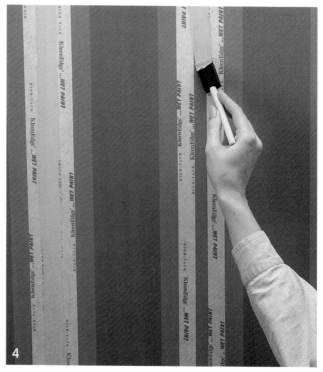

DIAGONAL STRIPES AND GEOMETRIC SHAPES decorate small accessories. Strips and cutouts of masking tape guide the painting.

TIPS FOR PAINTING TAPED-OFF DESIGNS

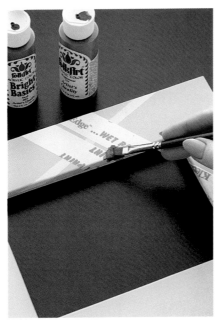

CUT geometric designs from painter's masking tape; apply to the surface over the base coat, pressing edges of tape firmly. Apply paint in a contrasting color; allow paint to dry. Remove the masking tape to reveal designs.

APPLY two rows of masking tape to the surface over the base coat, pressing edges firmly; apply paint in a contrasting color between rows. Allow paint to dry; remove masking tape.

PLAID DESIGN is created by masking off rows with tape.

How to paint a plaid design

MATERIALS

- Painter's masking tape in desired width or widths.
- Low-luster or mid-sheen latex enamel, for base coat; latex or craft acrylic paints for remaining colors.
- Paintbrush or paint roller, for applying base coat.
- Sponge applicator.
- Plaid fabric, optional, for inspiration.

1. Apply a base coat of low-luster or mid-sheen latex enamel in the desired color. Allow to dry. For the walls, mark vertical plumb line and horizontal level line, using carpenter's level.

2. Apply painter's masking tape of desired widths to the surface in horizontal parallel rows, pressing edges firmly; use plaid fabric as a guide for spacing rows, if desired.

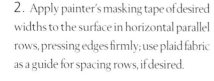

1

2

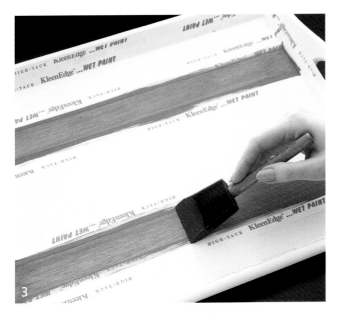

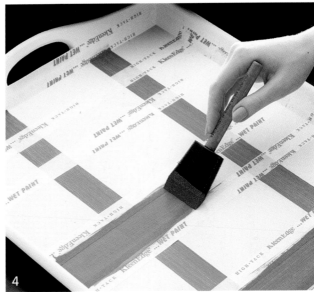

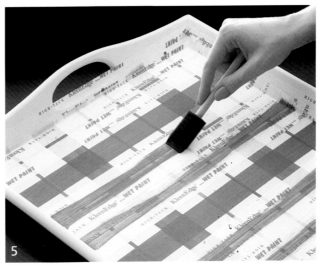

3. Thin paint so it gives translucent look. Apply a light coat of paint in the desired color to areas between the rows of tape. Pull a sponge applicator from one end to the other in a continuous motion, making fine lines in paint that simulate fabric weave. Allow to dry; remove tape.

4. Apply painter's masking tape to surface in vertical parallel rows, pressing the edges firmly. Apply the same paint color in opposite direction, between rows of tape.

5. Apply horizontal rows of masking tape for next color as in step 2; paint as in step 3. Then apply the masking tape for vertical rows, and apply same paint color.

6. Repeat the process for horizontal and vertical rows of each paint color.

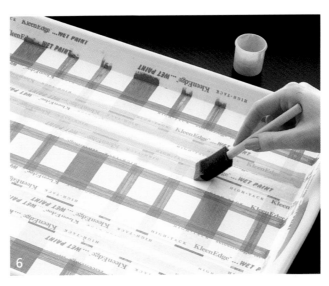

Stamped Designs

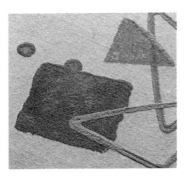

Use a basic stamping technique to create random designs. The paint was applied to the three designs shown here and on page 38 with everyday items like strips of cardboard, triangular makeup sponges, wooden blocks, a spaghetti lifter, and a bottle cork.

The coordinating designs are variations on a theme, and range in scale from small to medium to large. Select your favorite design, or use all three. When stamps are used to create several designs, you may choose to use the same colors, but in different ways. For example, the background color of one design may be used for one of the stamps in another design.

Experiment with the colors and the techniques on a large sheet of cardboard or on a remnant of fabric before you start the actual project.

MATERIALS

- ◆ Craft acrylic paints or fabric paints.
- ◆ Triangular makeup sponge and pieces of cardboard, for small stamped design.
- ◆ Square block of wood, cardboard, triangular makeup sponge, and wooden spaghetti lifter, for medium stamped design.
- ◆ Rectangular block of wood or foam, round bottle cork, cardboard, and rectangular eraser, for large stamped design.

How to paint a small stamped design

1. Apply first paint color to triangular makeup sponge; blot on paper towel. Stamp triangles onto surface, 3" to 4" (7.5 to 10 cm) apart. Allow to dry.

2. Cut a piece of cardboard about 1 1/2" (3.8 cm) long. Apply second paint color to edge of cardboard; blot. Stamp onto surface, varying the direction of the lines and overlapping the triangles; lines may also overlap. Allow to dry.

3. Cut a piece of cardboard about 2 1/2" (6.5 cm) long. Apply third paint color to edge; blot and stamp as in step 2.

How to paint a medium stamped design

1. Apply first paint color to wooden block; blot on paper towel. Stamp block prints onto surface, about 2" to 4" (5 to 10 cm) apart. Allow to dry.

2. Fold 5" (12.5 cm) piece of cardboard into triangle, and tape one corner together; sides of triangle do not need to be equal in length. Apply second paint color to the edge of triangle; blot. Stamp onto surface, varying the direction of the triangles and overlapping the block prints. Allow to dry.

3. Apply third paint color to triangular makeup sponge; blot. Stamp triangles onto surface, overlapping previous designs. Allow to dry.

4. Apply fourth paint color to spaghetti lifter; blot. Stamp onto surface, overlapping the previous designs.

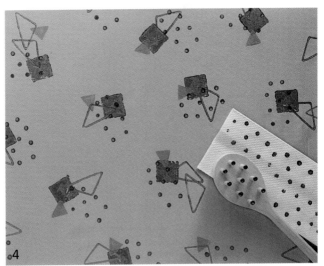

STAMPED DESIGNS, applied with every-day items like cardboard strips, wooden blocks, and corks, can be used on a single bold accessory, such as a toy chest.

How to paint a large stamped design

1. Apply first paint color to rectangular block of wood or foam; blot on paper towel. Stamp block prints onto surface, about 4" to 7" (10 to 18 cm) apart, varying the angles. Allow to dry.

2. Fold 12" (30.5 cm) piece of cardboard into triangle as in step 2 for medium stamped design, page 37. Apply second paint color to edge of triangle; blot. Stamp onto surface, varying the direction of the triangles and overlapping the block prints. Allow to dry.

3. Apply third paint color to round cork; blot. Stamp onto surface, overlapping block prints. Allow to dry.

4. Apply fourth paint color to one long edge of eraser; blot on paper towel, and stamp onto surface, overlapping the block prints. Allow to dry. Stamp with edge of cardboard as in step 2 for the small stamped design, page 36; stamp randomly in pairs.

FREEHAND DESIGNS

Easy Freehand Designs

Simple designs are easy to paint freehand, even if you do not consider yourself an artist. Discover many possible designs by looking at fabrics, wallcoverings, and gift-wrapping papers. When painting repetitive designs, you can allow the designs to vary slightly to emphasize the handmade quality, rather than painstakingly try to paint identical designs. Add interest to the painted pieces by using different designs to highlight separate areas of a single item.

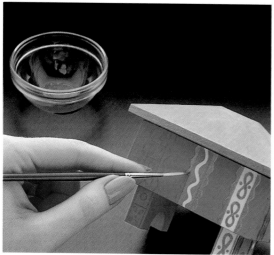

MARK simple freehand designs, using light pencil lines. Fill in the marked areas with paint, allowing the paint to dry between colors.

TRANSFER designs that are more intricate, using the methods on pages 23 to 27. Use appropriate artist's brush to fill in the design areas. When hand painting, you do not have to follow the marked design exactly.

*S*wirled Designs

Swirls of paint created with sweeping brush strokes make interesting designs. The three easy-to-copy designs shown here and on page 46 are created primarily with basic painting tools like artist's brushes, texture rollers, and paint pads. The designs range in scale from small to medium to large.

Paint the design on walls rather than use wallcoverings, or paint fabrics for unique accent pillows instead of selecting patterned fabrics. For small accessories, use smaller brushes and shorter brush strokes.

Vary the paint colors, selecting different colors for the different brush strokes. Keep in mind that dark and dull colors tend to recede while bright colors and metallic paints tend to advance. Metallic paints, which reflect light, add drama. For painting on fabrics, use the specialty paints intended for textiles (page 15).

When painting, overlap the brush strokes for a more layered, dimensional look. The spaces between the strokes can be varied slightly for interest. Experiment with the paint colors and techniques before you begin the actual project by painting on a large sheet of cardboard or on a remnant of fabric.

MATERIALS

- ◆ #4 round artist's brush, for small swirled design.
- ◆ #4 fan brush, #2 flat artist's brush, and #4 round artist's brush, for medium swirled design.
- ◆ 3" (7.5 cm) flat paintbrush, texture roller, and #4 round artist's brush, for large swirled design.
- ◆ Craft acrylic paints or fabric paints.
- ◆ Paint tray.

SWIRLED DESIGNS are made with brush strokes in several colors. These simple designs may be painted on walls as well as on fabrics.

How to paint a small swirled design

1. Apply the first paint color to surface in slightly curved brush strokes about 4" (10 cm) long and 4" to 6" (10 to 15 cm) apart, using #4 round artist's brush. Allow to dry.

2. Apply second color in curving brush strokes about 1½" (3.8 cm) long, using same brush; use less pressure on paintbrush so strokes are not as wide. Allow some strokes to overlap those of first color. Allow to dry.

3. Apply third color in curving strokes about 1" (2.5 cm) long, using tip of same brush. Allow some strokes to overlap the first color.

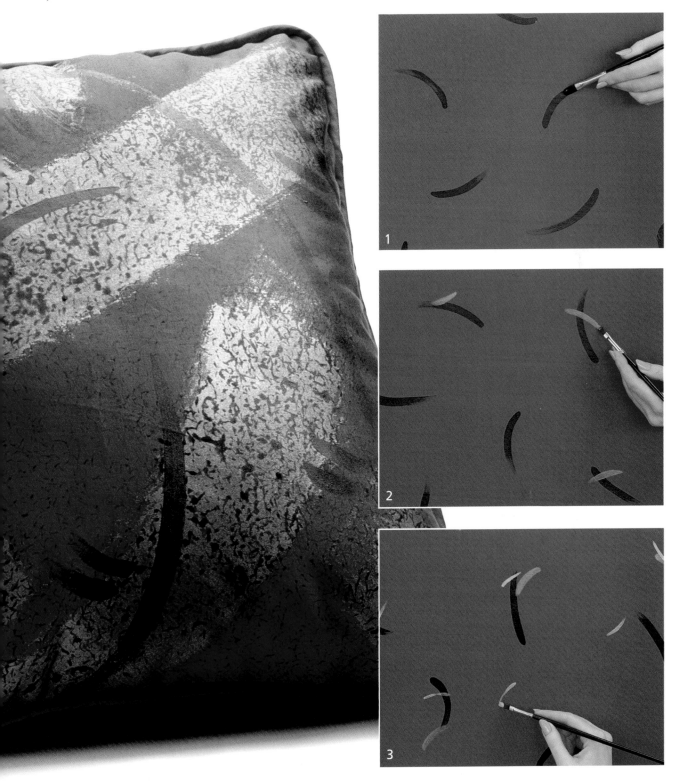

How to paint a medium swirled design

1. Apply first paint color to surface in brush strokes about 4" (10 cm) long, using fan brush. Allow to dry.

2. Apply the second color through middle of the first color in brush strokes about 6" (15 cm) long, using #2 flat artist's brush; vary the position for added interest. Allow to dry.

3. Apply third color in slightly curved brush strokes about 1½" to 2" (3.8 to 5 cm) long, using #4 round artist's brush. Allow to dry.

4. Wet the fan brush; blot on paper towel. Separate the bristles into small fingers. Dip into fourth paint color ¼" (6 mm), keeping bristles separated. Apply to surface in short brush strokes, about 1" (2.5 cm) long, applying light pressure.

How to paint a large swirled design

1. Dilute first paint color, one part paint to two parts water. Using 3″ (7.5 cm) paintbrush, apply paint to surface in slightly curved brush strokes, from 7″ to 14″ (18 to 35.5 cm) long. Allow to dry.

2. Dilute second paint color, one part paint to one part water; spread a thin layer in paint tray. Apply paint to texture roller; blot onto paper, then roll onto surface, overlapping the brush strokes from step 1. Allow to dry.

3. Apply the third color in curving brush strokes about 6″ to 12″ (15 to 30.5 cm) long, using #4 round artist's brush; overlap the brush strokes from step 1. Allow to dry.

4. Apply fourth color in pairs of short brush strokes, using #4 round artist's brush; overlap the edges of the strokes from step 1.

ABOVE: STENCILED TILES of this table-top were painted with ceramic paint. The ceramic paints were then heat-hardened before the ceramic tiles were installed.

LEFT: FAUX ONYX LAMP was painted with a primer recommended for use on glossy surfaces, then painted with a faux onyx finish, using craft acrylic paint.

Painting Ceramics

Glazed ceramics can be hand-painted to coordinate with the decorating scheme of a room. In order to paint on ceramics, it is important that you either prepare the surface by applying a primer recommended for glossy surfaces or that you use the specialty paints designed for ceramic painting. With either method, there is no need to sand the surface to degloss it before painting.

If you use a primer recommended for glossy surfaces, such as a stain-killing primer (page 9), the ceramic piece may be painted using latex or craft acrylic paint; glossy paints are recommended if you want to retain the sheen of glazed ceramic. The paint adheres well to the ceramic, provided the correct primer is used.

For another method of painting ceramics, use one of the ceramic paints that can be applied directly to the glazed ceramic without the use of a primer. These water-based paints, such as Liquitex® Glossies™ and DEKA®-Gloss, are heat-hardened in a low-temperature oven to further improve the ceramic paint's durability, adhesion, and water resistance.

Ceramic paints produce a hand-painted look, often with an uneven coverage that becomes part of the unique character of each piece. They vary in transparency, and some are easier to work with if they are thinned; for maximum durability, dilute the paints with a clear paint medium that is designed for use with ceramic paint. You may also want to spread the paints thinly, allowing the brush strokes to show, to emphasize the hand-painted quality of the design.

Use ceramic paints for display items, such as vases or decorative plates. Although ceramic paints are nontoxic, they are not recommended for use on eating or drinking utensils where food will come into contact with the paint. For best results, hand wash the painted ceramics in lukewarm water with mild detergent.

Two methods for painting glazed ceramics

PRIMER AND LATEX OR CRAFT ACRYLIC PAINT METHOD (A). Apply a primer that is recommended for glossy surfaces; allow to dry. Paint over the primer, using latex or craft acrylic paint; any of the painting techniques recommended for latex or craft acrylic paint can be used.

CERAMIC PAINT METHOD (B). Use ceramic paint, applying it directly to glazed ceramic surface; use desired painting technique, such as stenciling. Allow to dry. Heat-harden the paint in a low-temperature oven, following the manufacturer's directions.

More ideas for painting ceramics

TOP, RIGHT: COLOR-WASHED CERAMIC TEAPOT was painted with a fan brush. To achieve this effect, apply ceramic paint sparingly in cross-hatching brush strokes.

TOP, LEFT: SWIRLED DESIGNS (page 45) accent clear glass votives and a coordinating napkin ring. Ceramic paints were used for this technique.

LEFT: OLD CANISTERS are given a new look by painting them with a primer suitable for glossy surfaces, then with latex paint. Easy freehand designs (page 42) add a cheerful touch.

ABOVE: GOLD METALLIC DESIGN is painted on the wall at the head of the bed. Small fleur-de-lis motifs painted randomly on the walls support the decorating theme.

LEFT: SYMMETRICALLY DESIGNED GREEK COLUMNS painted on the wall visually support the shelf. The swag and tassel border is painted at picture-rail level.

Freehand Painted Designs for Walls

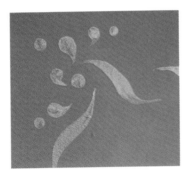

Freehand painting is a speedy way to add eye-catching interest to plain painted walls. Designs can range from stately architectural details to fanciful motifs. Simple symmetrical designs in one color are easiest to paint, while asymmetrical designs or designs with multiple colors may take a little preplanning. Use some of the designs shown here, or look for inspiration in wallpaper patterns, clip-art books, or stencils.

Craft acrylic paints or latex wall paints can be used for freehand painting. Acrylic paints, available in smaller quantities, may be more economical, depending on the size of the project. If a paint color is mixed, be sure to mix enough paint ahead of time to complete the entire project. Use wide, flat paintbrushes to paint bold lines; use other artist's brushes in styles and sizes necessary to achieve the desired look.

Allow the painted designs to be imperfect; that is part of the charm of freehand painting. To gain confidence, practice designs on tagboard or craft paper taped to the wall with masking tape.

MATERIALS

- ◆ Craft acrylic paint or latex wall paint.
- ◆ Paintbrushes in desired sizes and styles.
- ◆ Masking tape.
- ◆ Yardstick or carpenter's level, for marking guides as necessary.

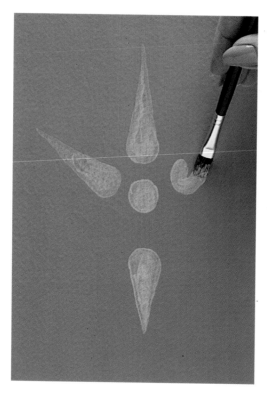

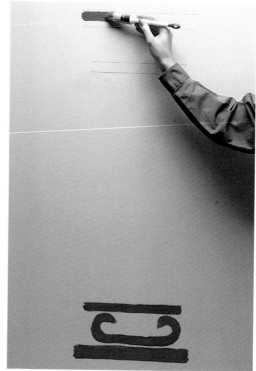

SYMMETRICAL MOTIFS. Paint the center of the design first; then paint small sections of the design on either side of the center, working outward until entire design is complete.

BORDERS. Mark guide points on wall, using yardstick or carpenter's level, before painting evenly spaced swags or wavy lines. Keep the brush moving at a constant, rhythmic pace across the wall, redipping brush in paint as necessary. Fill in details after entire border is laid out.

LARGE DESIGNS. Mark faint pencil guidelines on the wall at strategic points in large designs. Paint dominant details first to anchor design on wall; then paint secondary design lines to complete design.

RANDOM MOTIFS. Mark placement for motifs, using small pieces of masking tape, before beginning to paint. Vary sizes or colors for added interest, if desired.

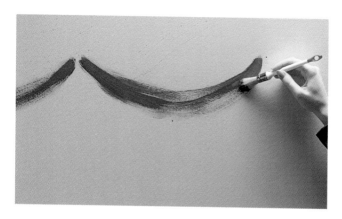

More ideas for freehand designs

RIGHT: CONTEMPORARY ASYMMET-
RICAL DESIGN painted on the wall boldly
outlines a window. Small motifs taken from
the design are painted randomly on the wall,
unifying the room.

BELOW: FAUX BRICKWORK painted
on the wall under a shelf resembles a fire-
place and mantel. Faux brickwork chair rail
continues around the room.

Continued

PAINT different designs in each section of the legs of a table or the turned posts of a headboard.

OPPOSITE: BRIGHTLY PAINTED TABLE is a cheerful accent for a child's room.

ABOVE: HEADBOARD is creatively painted for a personalized, whimsical effect.

BELOW: CERAMIC PAINTS are used to create a one-of-a-kind decorative bowl.

MARK a grid onto the surface, using a pencil; paint along the lines, using a liner brush. Fill in the areas with a random, light application of paint.

Continued

More ideas for freehand designs
(CONTINUED)

UNFINISHED MEDICINE CABINETS,
available at unpainted-furniture stores, can be
decoratively painted with stylized designs.

ABOVE: WALL DISPLAY features a shelf with freehand designs and stenciled wall designs. The ceramics are decorated with freehand designs combined with sponge painting; specialty ceramic paints were used.

BELOW: WOODEN STOOL is given new life with painted leaf designs.

TRACE around simple patterns, using a pencil. Fill in the areas with paint; allow to dry. Then add details with contrasting colors.

Index

CY DECOSSE INCORPORATED

President/COO: Nino Tarantino
Executive V.P./Editor-in-Chief: William B. Jones
Chairman Emeritus: Cy DeCosse

Creative Touches™
Group Executive Editor: Zoe A. Graul
Managing Editor: Elaine Johnson
Editor: Linda Neubauer
Associate Creative Director: Lisa Rosenthal
Senior Art Director: Delores Swanson
Art Director: Mark Jacobson
Copy Editor: Janice Cauley
Desktop Publishing Specialist: Laurie Kristensen
Sample Production Manager: Carol Olson
Photo Studio Services Manager: Marcia Chambers
Publishing Production Manager: Kim Gerber

President/COO: Philip L. Penny

PAINTED DESIGNS ETC.
Created by: The Editors of Cy DeCosse Incorporated

Also available in the Creative Touches™ series:

Stenciling Etc., Sponging Etc., Stone Finishes Etc.,
Valances Etc., Metallic Finishes Etc., Swags Etc.,
Papering Projects Etc.

The Creative Touches™ series draws from the individual titles of
The Home Decorating Institute®. Individual titles are also available
from the publisher and in bookstores and fabric stores.

Printed on American paper by:
  R. R. Donnelley & Sons Co.
99 98 97 96 / 5 4 3 2 1

Cy DeCosse Incorporated offers a variety of how-to books.

For information write:
  Cy DeCosse Subscriber Books
  5900 Green Oak Drive
  Minnetonka, MN 55343